Sandy Ground Boat Men

Written by Avenella K. Griffith

Illustrated by Navene Mairyshaw & Carmel Gumbs

Printed in the United States of America
First Edition: 2020

ISBN 13: 978-1-949105-30-8 (Paperback)
ISBN 13: 978-1-949105-31-5 (Hardback)
ISBN 13: 978-1-949105-32-2 (eBook)

Divine Works Publishing, LLC
Royal Palm Beach, Florida USA

www.DivineWorksPublishing.com
561-990-BOOK (2665)

CONTENTS

INTRODUCTION

Boat Men - the first book in the Sandy Ground Tales Series.

This is a compilation of two exciting and uniquely illustrated stories filled with creatively woven images and facts.

From the shores of Sandy Ground Anguilla, **Boat Men** sails through the real life motivational stories of David Carty and Garfield Richardson.

Bathed in humour and pivoting around the themes of resilience, cultural preservation, and entrepreneurship, the book resounds with the core Anguillian values of hard work, determination, and commitment.

Boat Men possesses the capacity to inspire the young, engage the academic, intrigue the philosopher, excite the historian, and catch leisurely readers hook, line, and sinker.

A Boat Builder

The Rebel

Illustrated by Navene Mairyshaw

David grew up around the sea...
Sandy Ground sea mainly.

His grandfadder, great grandfadder (you get the point),
Were all fishermen or boat captains.

In fact, he studied everything.

After excelling in Sixth Form, he got a university scholarship (that is another story for another day).

On returning to Anguilla (after trying other options), David became a teacher, a very good one too.

Then, in 1979, he was moved to Director of Tourism and things were going good, real good...

Then the
political party
in power
changed and
"I tell ya, all
hell broke
loose!"
He was fired!

The civil servants went on strike! (First time ever).

unfair

"This is unfair!" they cried. For not quelling them, David was considered the leader of the rebellion.

Now David had no job and had a new young wife and a son. What would he do? It's a man's job to provide for his family.

He scratched his head (right there on the right side), and thought and thought and thought.

One fore day morning, when ideas usually came to him, he decided to resort to becoming a fisherman.

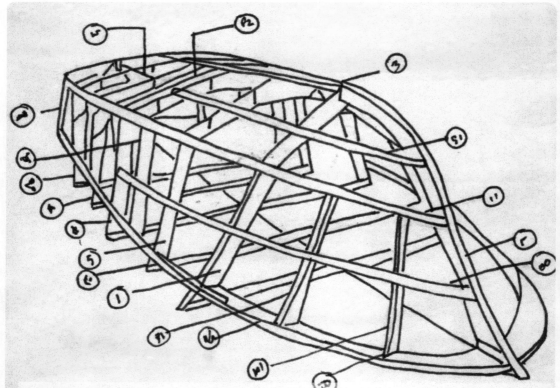

So with what he had inherited through 'genes', gathered from books and helping his grandfather, he set out to build a boat (that's a whole 'nother story too).

He was proud of
himself when it was
done.

Fueled with some anger, and in a moment of genius, he named it "Rebel".

But after one single solitary trip out fishing jus' off Miss Anguilla land, Saga Boy David knew earning a living on the sea was not for him! He had no sea legs! LOL!

So he hauled her up!
His speed and comfort was gone
again like a UFO.

He slowly raised his Ebenezer and scratched his head again (right there on the right side). What was he going to do? He had a family to feed. He had to Press On and don't give up.

A few days passed and no ideas were coming at foreday morning. One day a guy came walking through the bush, like a Village Ram, and met David under De Tree.

He handed David a brown paper bag and said, "Daddy say tek dis money. He want to buy de boat ya jus' buil'."

HUHHHHHH???
Mi SONNNNNN! Dis was Decision time!

Absent minded of the Wasp nest above, David scratched his head (the whole head dis time, right side and then on top). Light 'n Peace had shown up!

There was $2000 in the bag!

David quickly did the math and realized that this opportunity before him was indeed the Real Deal.

Quick like the sonic,

David said, "Yes".

The next foreday morning, the big superstar idea was pretty much formed in David's head. Today, we see it as Rebel Marine!

FYI

In 1984 Rebel Marine built 'Two Cheers'. It was the first daily high speed ferry boat to run between Anguilla and St. Martin. It operated on the hour. In its first year, it clocked over 100,000 miles going forward and backward between the channel.

Prior to Two Cheers, people had to jump on and sit on the floor of the Silver Still, along with the pigs, goats, sheep, cows and chickens. It left AXA at 8:00 a.m. and returned from SXM at 12 noon (miss it and ya had to sleep over dere until de next day). The journey was an hour long (lolol we come far, boy).

Mind Games

- List five (5) other boats built by Rebel Marine.

- Write down the names of all the local sailing boats in the story.

- Research some names of local boats not currently sailing.

Morals of the Story

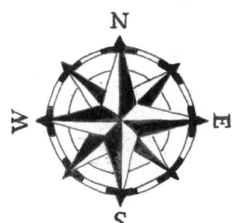

1. When one door closes another door opens (but there's hell in the hallways)!

2. ....

3. ....

4. ....

A Boat Lover

Gotcha!

Illustrated by Carmel Gumbs and Navene Mairyshaw

Back in de day, every Anguillian boy used to dream about owning his own boat... a fishing boat.

Garfield dreamt too, but he wanted a different boat; he wanted a charter boat.

A boat business to take people around to Anguilla's beautiful beaches and cays is what he dreamed of.

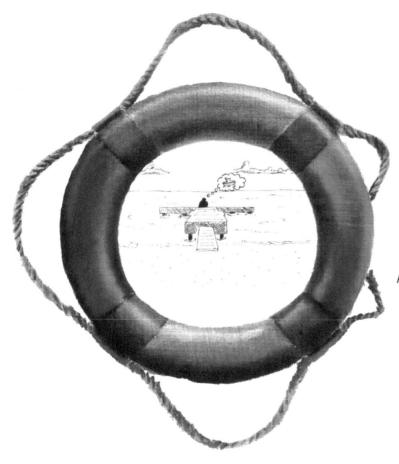

In school he dreamed.

At home he dreamed.

At Sandy Ground beach he dreamed even more.

Garfield became a bartender on the beautiful Sandy Island. Everybody loved Garfield and his extra extra large smile. They liked his drinks too.

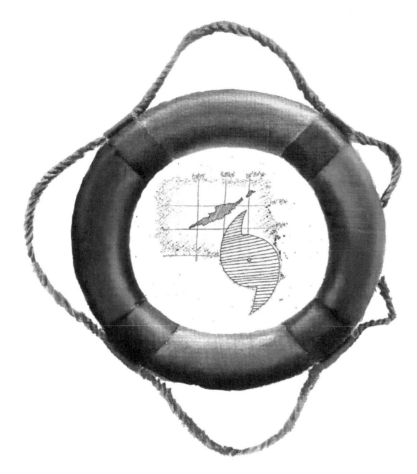

Then one day
in 1995
something bad
happened....

Hurricane Luis
made a direct
hit on
Anguilla.

The restaurant on Sandy Island was gone.
In fact, Sandy itself was gone!
Completely gone!

What would
Garfield do
now?

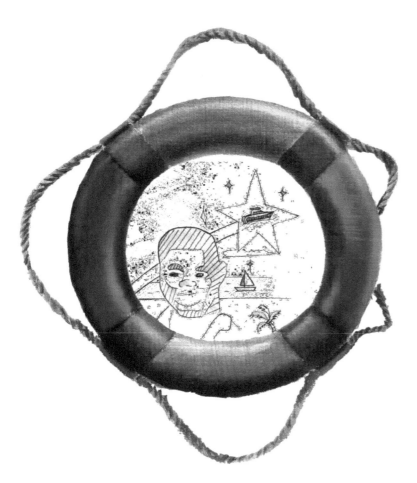

"I'll go for my dream and get my boat!" he decided.

"What do I have to lose?"

"Certainly my father would help me..." he thought to himself.

"No! I'm not helping you with that foolish, struppid idea... it will never never wuk!" his father Bertie shouted. "It makes absolutely no sense and it will never wuk!"

Deeply disappointed, but with even more determination, Garfield had another idea.

To CCB he went......and the manager, knowing his hard work ethic, gave him a loan.... just like a dat.

With money in hand, Garfield went straight to Rebel Marine and a transaction was made.

(All without
Garfield's
father
knowing).

When the boat was ready to leave the boat yard in North Hill, Garfield climbed up the trailer and jumped on board.

Into Sandy Ground it descended and Garfield's heart was pumping.......He would soon be passing his father's souvenir shop (right next to the Methodist Church)..

And there he was, standing black and tall in the door way...... mouth open with shock as he read both Garfield's extra extra wide smile and the name of the boat which said the same thing.......

GOTCHA!

The Fleet

GOTCHA

GOTCHA AGAIN

GOTCHA TOO

GOTCHA REEL GOOD

GOTCHA Summertime

GOTCHA Summer Breeze

GOTCHA It's Summer Again

Morals of the Story

1. When one door closes another door opens (but there's hell in the hallways)!

2. ....

3. ....

4. ....

About The Scribe

With roots in Sandy Ground and a continued affiliation with the village, Avenella Griffith has a high appreciation for its milieu.

She tells these Tales in a drive to capture, for generations to come, the lives and stories of some of the people who have shaped the village.

The preservation of Anguilla's great history, traditions and people through inspirational writings is her broader motivation for this work.

Amongst other things, Avenella also hopes that through the Tales, young people, especially boys, would enjoy reading, would dream and be inspired to work hard to achieve their dreams.

CPSIA information can be obtained
at www.ICGtesting.com
Printed in the USA
JSHW051552150421
13599JS00001B/1